PROFESSOR PRONG
and the Great Puzzle-Solving Machine

Eva Mills

Illustrated by Greg Wold

Momentum

Professor Prong and the Great Puzzle-Solving Machine

First published in Great Britain in 1999 by

Folens Publishers
Albert House
Apex Business Centre
Boscombe Road
Dunstable
Beds LU5 4RL

© 1999 Momentum developed by Barrie Publishing Pty Limited
Suite 513, 89 High St, Kew, Vic 3101, Australia

Eva Mills hereby asserts her moral right to be identified as the author of this work in accordance with the Copyright, Designs and Patents Act 1988.
© 1999 Folens Ltd. on behalf of the author.
Illustrations copyright Greg Wold.

All rights reserved. No part of this publication may be reproduced or transmitted in any form or by any means, electronic or mechanical, including photocopying, recording or any information storage and retrieval system, without written permission from the publisher.

British Library Cataloguing in Publication Data.
A Catalogue record for this book is available from the British Library

ISBN 1 86202 735 8

Designed by Tom Kurema
Printed in Singapore by PH Productions Pte Ltd

Nick stood outside Professor Prong's house and looked at the brass plaque fixed to the wall beside the door:

C. J. Prong
Mechanical Engineer and Puzzle Solver

The plaque glinted in the sunlight, as bright and shiny as a new coin.

Ever since Professor Prong had moved into the house next door, strange noises kept Nick awake at night: bumping and hammering and drilling and dragging noises. Nick was certain Professor Prong was building something, but what could it be?

Suddenly the front door opened and the professor appeared.

"Morning, Nick," he said. "Any puzzles for me to solve today?"

"No, Professor," said Nick, looking down at the ground. "I was just on my way to school."

Professor Prong breathed heavily through his nose. "I was just on the way to breakfast myself."

He walked away down the street, and Nick followed carefully some distance behind.

Professor Prong strolled along with a slow, even stride that was surprisingly hard to keep up with. His whitish hair stuck out in all directions, stiff and straight. He had a long bumpy nose that seemed to lead him down the street. As Nick watched him bump into pedestrians and bounce off a street sign, he decided Professor Prong must be nearsighted as well.

Nick saw the professor stop at a newsstand and buy the morning paper. He saw him go into Mario's Cafe and sit at the table by the window. He saw him open the paper and study the crossword puzzle. And then Nick saw Professor Prong order eggs Benedict and strong black coffee.

I wonder if what he's building has something to do with crosswords and eggs Benedict? thought Nick.

Nick learned some interesting things at school that day, but the most absorbing was the Riddle of the Sphinx.

"In ancient Greek mythology," explained Ms Tyler, "the Sphinx was a monster with the head of a woman, the body of a lion and the wings of an eagle. The Sphinx would not let anyone pass by unless they could solve this riddle: What goes on four legs in the morning, two legs in the daytime and three legs in the evening?"

Nick sat and thought about the riddle, but he couldn't think of any animal that sometimes uses four legs, sometimes two legs and sometimes three legs.

"Is it a three-legged dog?" asked Brigid.

"Is it a horse when it's trotting, and then cantering, and then galloping?" asked Jack.

"Is it a dancing elephant?" asked Gina.

Ms Tyler just laughed and shook her head. "The answer is a human being. When we are born, we crawl around on four legs. When we are grown, we walk on two legs. When we are old, we use a walking stick, so we have three legs!"

A few groans broke out around the class. "That's hard, Ms Tyler," said Gina.

"Yes, it is," said Ms Tyler. "The first person ever to solve the Riddle of the Sphinx was Oedipus, a character in Greek mythology."

"Why does the riddle talk about the times of the day when it was really about a person's life?" asked Nick.

"That's the way a riddle works," explained Ms Tyler. "Sometimes words that seem to mean one thing really mean something else."

Now that he knew the answer, Nick thought the riddle was actually easy. Maybe that was another way riddles worked.

"I'll give you another riddle to take home," said Ms Tyler. "You can ask for help if you want to. I'd like you to have some sort of answer tomorrow, even if it's just a guess. The riddle is: What will grow if you give it food, and die if you give it water?"

Nick walked home from school and thought about the riddle. All animals would grow if you gave them food, but he couldn't think of one that would die if you gave it water. He couldn't think of anything. He didn't have a clue. He was sure everyone would think he was really stupid.

At home he told his mother the riddle. She scratched her head and frowned a little.

"Could it be something that lives in the desert where there is not much water? Like a camel? Or a snake? Or a cactus?" Nick's mother screwed up her nose and wiggled her tongue and pulled at her ear, but none of that helped.

"I have to come up with an answer!" wailed Nick. "I can't be the only one in class without a solution!"

"Well ..." said his mother slowly. "If it's that important to you, I suppose we could go next door and ask Professor Prong."

Nick rang the doorbell. From inside the house came the sound of long, slow footsteps. The door opened and there stood Professor Prong.

"Afternoon, Nick," he said. "Any puzzles for me to solve today?"

"Yes," said Nick. "I've got a riddle to solve for school."

Inside, the small house was dark and cool. It smelled of grease and iron filings and wood shavings. Nick followed the professor down a long, narrow hallway.

The hallway opened out into a large, bright room. The entire space was taken up with the biggest, weirdest, most complicated-looking machine Nick had ever seen.

The machine was the size of a small bus. It was covered with wires and flashing buttons and video screens, all held together by a flimsy-looking metal frame. Nick saw six CD players stacked one above the other. There were three modems and four laptop computers. There was even a video camera. Its lens peered down at Nick.

"This," said Professor Prong proudly, "is Prong's Patented Puzzle-Solving Machine! It's only Mark I, of course — a prototype at this stage."

"Does that mean it's still being tested?" asked Nick.

"Indeed it does," snorted the professor. "But I think I have nearly perfected the mechanism. Let me demonstrate."

He grabbed two newspapers from a stack in the corner of the room. "Here is yesterday's crossword puzzle, not yet completed," he said, waving a page of the newspaper in front of Nick. "And here is the solution from this morning's paper."

He handed the solution page to Nick, and moved over to a part of the machine that looked suspiciously like a normal office photocopier.

"Now, watch!" he said. He lifted the lid of the photocopier and placed yesterday's blank crossword puzzle on the glass, then pressed the copy button. The photocopier whirred into life, and its bright light moved across the entire puzzle. Nick waited for a photocopy to appear at one end.

Instead, the whole enormous puzzle-solving machine gave a great groan and began buzzing and flashing and beeping. The machine shuddered and shook, and just when Nick thought the whole thing was going to collapse on top of them, there was a loud Ping! The machine wound down slowly, until only the photocopier was still whirring away. Out of the end of the machine a piece of paper appeared, which Professor Prong snatched up and presented to Nick proudly.

"Compare the machine's answer with the solution!" he said. "Are they the same, or are they the same?"

Nick looked from the printed solution to the answer from the machine. They were indeed identical.

"Wow!" he said. "It really works!"

The Professor smiled. "Now, Nick, what is your puzzle?"

"It's a riddle," said Nick. "What will grow if you give it food, and die if you give it water?"

"A riddle!" exclaimed Professor Prong. "Excellent! I have not yet tested my machine for riddles. First we must write it down and then pass it to the machine."

He wrote down the riddle on a blank piece of paper and placed it on the photocopier.

"Now, watch!" he said. He pressed the copy button and stood back. The photocopier whirred into life. Its bright light moved across the page on the glass. The whole enormous puzzle-solving machine gave a great groan and began buzzing and flashing and beeping. The machine shuddered and shook and whined and moaned. The noise grew louder and louder until Nick had to shout to be heard.

"Why is it taking so long this time?" he asked.

"It is searching through all its memory banks for the solution," Professor Prong said. "It will take a little longer because it has never seen a riddle before."

Suddenly there was a bang! A stream of smelly black smoke poured out of one of the CD players. The machine's whine turned into a high-pitched whistle. There was so much shuddering and shaking going on that the whole room was vibrating.

Professor Prong waved his arms at Nick. "You'd better get out!" he shouted. "I think it's going to blow!"

Nick stumbled down the hallway and out onto the footpath, coughing and sputtering through the smoke.

Nick could still hear the piercing whine of the machine. Clouds of foul-smelling smoke were billowing out the front door.

Suddenly there was a loud crackle and a pop, and a flash of light from inside the house, and — KABOOM!

The explosion knocked Nick flat on his back. The windows of Professor Prong's house shattered and glass sprayed out into the street. An enormous cloud of smoke and dust whooshed out the front door.

Nick picked himself up slowly. His ears were ringing and his eyes were stinging from the smoke. He looked at the house. The new brass plaque still glinted in the sunlight, and everything was silent. In the distance Nick could make out the sound of an approaching fire engine.

Poor Professor Prong, thought Nick. Now I'll never find an answer to my riddle.

Then Professor Prong staggered out the front door and onto the street. He was black from head to foot, and his hair was sticking out even more than usual.

"It works!" he yelled excitedly. "It works!"

Nick's mother rushed out of their house and back up the street.

"Are you okay?" she called.

"Can't hear a thing!" the professor shouted. "But it works!"

A bright red fire engine came roaring up the street. It screeched to a stop, and firefighters jumped out. An ambulance arrived a minute later. An ambulance officer took Professor Prong gently by the arm. "He'll be fine, but we'll take him to the hospital for observation," she said.

As he was led away, Professor Prong continued to point at the house and shout gleefully, "It works! It works!"

Nick watched as the firefighters turned their hoses on the house. Rivers of water began to quench the flames. Suddenly his eyes lit up. "That's it!" he cried. "The professor's machine has given us the answer, after all."

"What do you mean?" asked Nick's mother.

"The answer to the riddle," Nick said. "What will grow if you give it food, and die if you give it water?" He pointed towards the smoking house. "Fire."